SOUS VIDE
SUMMER RECIPES

Easy, Fresh and Tasty Summer Recipes for Perfectly Cooking Restaurant-Quality food

Sophia Marchesi

IPPOCERONTE
publishing

**Copyright © 2021 by Sophia Marchesi
All rights reserved**

This document is geared towards providing exact and reliable information with regards to the topic and issue covered. The publication is sold with the idea that the publisher is not required to render accounting, officially permitted, or otherwise, qualified services. If advice is necessary, legal or professional, a practiced individual in the profession should be ordered.

From a Declaration of Principles which was accepted and approved equally by a Committee of the American Bar Association and a Committee of Publishers and Associations.

In no way is it legal to reproduce, duplicate, or transmit any part of this document in either electronic means or in printed format. Recording of this publication is strictly prohibited and any storage of this document is not allowed unless with the written permission from the publisher. All rights reserved.

The information provided herein is stated to be truthful and consistent, in that any liability, in terms of inattention or otherwise, by any usage or abuse of any policies, processes, or directions contained within is the solitary and utter responsibility of the recipient reader. Under no circumstances will any legal responsibility or blame be held against the publisher for any reparation, damages, or monetary loss due to the information herein, either directly or indirectly.

Respective authors own all copyrights not held by the publisher.

The information herein is offered for informational purposes solely and is universal as so. The presentation of the information is without a contract or any type of guarantee assurance.

The trademarks that are used are without any consent, and the publication of the trademark is without permission or backing by the trademark owner. All trademarks and brands within this book are for clarifying purposes only and are owned by the owners themselves, not affiliated with this document.

CONTENTS

INTRODUCTION 7
RECIPES 11
  1. Lemon Hummus 12
  2. A Bed of Vegetables... 14
  3. Tomato And Mango Salsa 16
  4. Shrimp and Avocado Salsa 18
  5. Garlic Corn and Herby 20
  6. Nuts, Beetroot and Cheese Salad 22
  7. Brioche and Eggs 24
  8. Citrus Yogurt.. 26
  9. Orange Yogurt.. 28
  10. Dungeness Crab 29
  11. Zucchini Medallions 30
  12. Summer Salsa 32
  13. Coconut and Almond Porridge 33
  14. Glazed Carrots.. 34
  15. Hot Chili Chutney 36
  16. Eggs with Avocado Toast 38
  17. Cinnamon Eggs 40
  18. Asparagus.. 41
  19. Lemon Flavored Scallops 42
  20. Tomatoes... 44
  21. Colorful Bell Pepper Mix 46
  22. Artichokes.. 48
  23. Filipino Adobo Chicken....................................... 49
  24. Mediterranean Eggplant Lasagna 50
  25. Barbecue Chicken 52

26. Lemon Pork Chops 54
27. Burgers 56
28. Spicy Honey Sriracha Wings 58
29. Fresh Herb Rubbed Pork Chops 60
30. Juicy Orange Duck Breast 62
31. Crunchy Coconut Shrimps 64
32. Haddock on Vegetable Sauce 66
33. Lobster Tail 68
34. Sea Bass 70
35. Cajun Spiced Tilapia 72
36. Brined Salmon 74
37. Marinated King Prawns with Lime Mayonnaise 76
38. Cilantro Curried Zucchinis 78
39. Beef Shogayaki 80
40. Vanilla Pears 82
41. Peach 84
42. Rose Water Apricots 86
43. Peach and Orange Jam 87
44. Pineapple in Malibu 88
45. Sweet Corn Cheesecake 90
46. Bananas Foster 92
47. Vanilla Ice Cream 94
48. Feisty Kiwi and Vanilla 96
49. Juicy Raspberries 98
50. Mini Cheesecakes 100

TEMPERATURE CHARTS 102
COOKING CONVERSION 108
RECIPE INDEX 112

INTRODUCTION

In this book, I have collected a selection of my favorite summer recipes, some are re-elaborations of classic recipes that I used to do with my family when I was younger, others are the result of my travels around the world. Each recipe in this book evokes a memory of an important moment in my life, so I hope you will enjoy them.

Cooking is something that runs in my blood, most of my food memories are of my Nan cooking Sunday dinners - lasagna and cannelloni to share with the whole family. When I was young, I have never liked to be stuck in a classroom, I started culinary school at a very young age, and the only thing I really wanted was to be out cooking. You could say I was not a particularly good student, but I have always been really passionate about food.

I have been working in a professional kitchen since I was seventeen years old and I'm running my own restaurant since I was 23. The past thirty years have been a rewarding, yet arduous journey that I spent learning the basics and mastering the different cuisines and techniques by taking the best out of each of them. It was last year, during the lockdown, that I realized that I was starting to lose my passion. Preparing a dish had become an aseptic and mechanical where perfection was king.

I wanted to go back to my roots, cooking has always been about my family; preparing a dish together with the people I love gives me time to connect and create precious memories. Setting aside a time where the entire family can work together to create a meal gives us a chance to pause, catch up and just connect with each other.

What I would like to share with you in this book is my renewed passion and a technique that I learned during my time in France, the Sous Vide. This innovative cooking method is something my grandmother never thought existed and creates the perfect opportunity to spend some time in the kitchen with my family. For these reasons, I think the Sous Vide is the perfect combination of my professional and domestic life.

Sous Vide is the French term that translates to "under vacuum" and it is the method for preparing a dish at a specifically controlled temperature and time; your food should be prepared at the temperature at which it will be eaten. Put simply, this procedure involves placing food in vacuum seal bags and boiling it in a specially built bath of water for longer than average cooking times (usually 1 to 7 hours, up to 48 or more in some cases). Cooking at an exact temperature takes the guesswork out of the equation that defines a perfect meal. You can easily prepare your steak, chicken, lamb, pork, etc., exactly the way you like it, every single time.

It is easy to use and leads to great results every time. You will end up with food that is more tender and juicier than anything else you've ever made. This technique will help you to take your everyday cooking to a higher level. To do a top dish, most of the time, you do not need exotic ingredients, it is just a matter to get the best from the ingredients you already know.

The greatest part of Sous Vide cooking is that it does not require your constant presence in the kitchen. When the food is sealed in a bag and placed in the water bath, you can leave it at a low temperature, and it will cook on its own without asking much of your attention. The Sous Vide Cookers that are nowadays available in the market are efficient at regulating the perfect temperature to cook food according to its texture while maintaining the minimum required temperature. So, while your food is in the water, your hands are practically free to work on other important tasks or spend some quality time with your family.

It is an artful skill that is definitely worth trying. If it is just your first time, don't feel bad if you don't get the results you wanted to achieve. You will get better by gaining experience with this cookbook! The key is having patience, the right information, and consistency.

The meals prepared with Sous Vide are tasty and healthy, since this technique does not use added fats during the preparation of your dish also, using low temperature ensures that the perfect cooking point is reached.

Dishes included in this cookbook are simple, delicious, and provide you with so many options that you'll be preparing them for years to come. These recipes are made to be shared with the people you love and to build new precious food memories as I did with my Nan.

RECIPES

1. LEMON HUMMUS

Cal.: 225 | Fat: 6g | Protein: 6g

Preparation Time: 15 minutes
Cooking Time: 3 hours
Servings: 12

Ingredients

½ cup tahini, see our homemade tahini recipe
1/3 cup fresh lemon juice
1/4 cup extra-virgin olive oil
1 teaspoon cayenne pepper
Salt and black pepper, to taste
1 pound chickpeas
1 teaspoon onion powder
2 garlic cloves, smashed

Directions

1. In a deep and large bowl filled with water, put the chickpeas and leave to soak through the night.

2. Strain the chickpeas.

3. Prepare your sous-vide water bath to a tempera-

ture of 183°F/84°C.

4. Transfer the chickpeas into a cooking pouch with 4 cups of water.

5. Seal the pouch and immerse it in the preheated water bath.

6. Cook for 3 hours and 9 minutes.

7. Once done, transfer the cooked chickpeas to a food blender and blend them together with the remaining ingredients.

8. Serve and enjoy chilled!

2. A BED OF VEGETABLES

Cal.: 398 | Fat: 26g | Protein: 19g

Preparation Time: 9 minutes
Cooking Time: 48 minutes
Servings: 4

Ingredients

1 cucumber
3 carrots
1 sweet potato
1 red, green and yellow pepper each
1 leek
1 pinch each of chili powder, salt and pepper
1 tbsp. olive oil

Directions

1. Clean all vegetables, peel them if necessary, and cut them into bite-sized pieces. Marinate in a bowl with the oil, chili, pepper and salt.

2. Vacuum seal in a suitable bag.

3. Preheat the water bath to 185°F/85°C and let the vegetables cook for 40 minutes. This also works in the steamer.

4. Once removed from the bag, the vegetables are ready to be served on the plate.

5. Drape meat or fish on top and let the vegetables turn into a bed.

3. TOMATO AND MANGO SALSA

Cal.: 264 | Fat: 20g | Protein: 13g

Preparation Time: 16 minutes
Cooking Time: 11 minutes
Servings: 6

Ingredients

2 tablespoons extra-virgin olive oil
3 medium tomatoes, diced
2 large ripe mangos, peeled, pitted, and diced
1 medium red onion, diced
2 tablespoons chopped fresh cilantro
1 tablespoon minced fresh mint
Juice of 1 medium lime
1 tablespoon granulated sugar
½ teaspoon sea salt

Directions

1. Fill the water bath with water. Set your machine temperature to 150°F/65°C.

2. Place the oil, tomatoes, mangos and red onion in a food-safe bag and vacuum seal the bag.

3. Place the bag in the water bath and cook for 1 hour. Quick chill the bag by placing it in an ice bath.

4. Empty the bag into a large bowl and toss well with the remaining ingredients. Let the salsa marinate, in the refrigerator, for 10–15 minutes before serving.

4. SHRIMP AND AVOCADO SALSA

Cal.: 249 | Fat: 26g | Protein: 15g

Preparation Time: 11 minutes
Cooking Time: 1 hour 46 minutes
Servings: 6

Ingredients

1-pound raw medium shrimp, peeled and deveined
1 tablespoon olive oil
2 medium avocados, peeled, cored, and cubed
3 medium tomatoes, diced
2 medium jalapeño peppers, cored and minced
1/4 cup chopped fresh cilantro
Juice of 2 medium limes
½ teaspoon sea salt

Directions

1. Fill the water bath with water. Set your machine temperature to 140°F/60°C.

2. Place the shrimp and olive oil in a food-safe bag and vacuum seal the bag.

3. Place the shrimp in the water bath and cook for 30 minutes.

4. Remove the shrimp from the bag and cut each into 2–3 pieces.

5. In a large mixing bowl, combine all the ingredients and toss.

6. Let the salsa marinate, in the refrigerator, for 10–15 minutes before serving.

5. GARLIC CORN AND HERBY

Cal.: 397 | Fat: 37g | Protein: 6g

Preparation Time: 9 minutes
Cooking Time: 30 minutes
Servings: 6

Ingredients

1 teaspoon granulated garlic
1 tablespoon paprika
1 tablespoon fresh chives, chopped
6 ears corn
2 sticks butter, melted
1 teaspoon shallot powder
Flaked sea salt and white pepper, to taste

Directions

1. Prepare your sous-vide water bath to a temperature of 183°F/84°C.

2. Get the corn tossed with the entire ingredients.

3. Put the corn in a cooking pouch and seal after removing the excess air.

4. Immerse the pouch in the water bath and cook for 25 minutes.

5. Sprinkle with seasonings.

6. Serve and enjoy!

6. NUTS, BEETROOT AND CHEESE SALAD

Cal.: 127 | Fat: 7g | Protein: 7g

Preparation Time: 15 minutes
Cooking Time: 2 hours 30 seconds
Servings: 3

Ingredients

1 lb. Beetroot, peeled
½ cup Almonds, blanched
2 tbsp. Hazelnuts, skinned
2 tsp. Olive Oil
1 garlic clove, finely minced
1 tsp. Cumin Powder
1 tsp. Lemon Zest
Salt to taste
½ cup Goat Cheese, crumbled
Fresh Mint Leaves to garnish

Dressing:
2 tbsp. Olive Oil
1 tbsp. Apple Cider Vinegar

Directions

1. Make a water bath, place the cooker in it, and set at 183°F/84°C.

2. Cut the beetroots into wedges and bag in a vacuum-sealable bag.

3. Release air by the water displacement method, seal and Immerse the bag in the water bath and set the timer for 2 hours. Once the timer has stopped, remove and unseal the bag. Place the beetroot aside.

4. Put a pan over medium heat, add almonds and hazelnuts, and toast for 3 minutes. Transfer to a cutting board and chop.

5. Add oil to the same pan, add garlic and cumin. Cook for 30 seconds. Turn heat off. In a bowl, combine the goat cheese, almond mixture, and lemon zest and garlic mixture. Mix. Whisk olive oil and vinegar and place aside. Serve as a side dish.

7. BRIOCHE AND EGGS

Cal.: 397 | Fat: 34g | Protein: 19g

Preparation Time: 13 minutes
Cooking Time: 46 minutes
Servings: 6

Ingredients

6 brioche buns
6 large eggs
2 scallions, sliced (optional)
1 ½ cups grated cheese

Directions

1. Preheat the Sous Vide machine to 149°F/65°C.

2. Place the eggs on a spoon, one at a time, and gently lower them into the water bath and place on the rack. Set the timer for 45 minutes.

3. When the timer goes off, immediately remove the eggs from the water bath. Place the eggs in a bowl of cold water for a few minutes.

4. Place brioche buns on a baking sheet and break a cooked egg on each bun. Sprinkle cheese on top.

5. Set an oven to broil and place the baking sheet in the oven. Broil for a few minutes until the cheese melts.

8. CITRUS YOGURT

Cal.: 394 | Fat: 20g | Protein: 14g

Preparation Time: 12 minutes
Cooking Time: 3 hours
Servings: 8

Ingredients

1 cup yogurt
8 cups full cream milk
1 tablespoon grated orange zest
1 tablespoon grated lime zest
1 tablespoon grated lemon zest

Directions

1. Preheat the Sous Vide machine to 113°F/45°C.

2. Pour milk into a saucepan and place over medium heat. When the temperature of the milk reaches 180°F/82°C, turn off the heat. Let the milk cool to 110°F/43°C.

3. Add 2 tablespoons of yogurt in each of 8 canning jars. Divide the milk among the jars, then divide the zests among the jars and stir. Fasten the lid on the jars.

4. Immerse the filled jars in the water bath. The lids of the

jars should be above the level of water in the cooker.

5. Set the timer for 3 hours.

6. Remove from the water bath and cool completely. Refrigerate for a few hours before use.

9. ORANGE YOGURT

Cal.: 120 | Fat: 12g | Protein: 3g

Preparation Time: 11 minutes
Cooking Time: 4 hours
Servings: 4

Ingredients

4 cups milk
½ cup Greek yogurt
1 tbsp. orange zest
½ tbsp. lemon zest

Directions

1. Pour the milk into a pan and heat it to 180°F/82°C. Cool it down to the room temperature.

2. Preheat the water bath to 113°F/45°C.

3. Mix in the yogurt, add the orange and lemon zest and pour the mixture into canning jars.

4. Cover the jars with the lids and cook in the water bath for 3 hours.

5. When the time is up, cool down the jars to the room temperature and then refrigerate before serving.

10. DUNGENESS CRAB

Cal.: 309 | Fat: 45g | Protein: 20g

Preparation Time: 8 minutes
Cooking Time: 50 minutes
Servings: 4

Ingredients

1 Dungeness crab

Directions

1. Preheat the water bath to 154°F/68°C.

2. Bring a large pot of water to a boil.

3. Fully Immerse crab in boiling water for 1 minute to blanch.

4. Transfer crab to the steam cooker.

5. Cover with lid, and steam for 45 minutes.

6. Serve hot, or chill in an ice bath for 10 minutes to serve cold.

11. ZUCCHINI MEDALLIONS

Cal.: 133 | Fat: 11.9g | Protein: 2.5g

Preparation Time: 15 minutes
Cooking Time: 30 minutes
Servings: 2

Ingredients

2 zucchinis, sliced
2 tablespoons butter
Salt and black pepper, to taste

Directions

1. Prepare and preheat the water bath at 185°F/85°C.

2. Add zucchini and all the ingredients to a zipper-lock bag.

3. Seal the zipper-lock bag using the water immersion method.

4. Place the sealed bag in the bath and cook for 30 minutes.

5. Once done, transfer the zucchini along with the sauce to a plate.

6. Serve.

12. SUMMER SALSA

Cal.: 155 | Fat: 0.6g | Protein: 5.6g

Preparation Time: 10 minutes
Cooking Time: 30 minutes
Servings: 10

Ingredients

2 cans of sweet corn (yellow or white)
1 can of black beans
½ red onion, chopped
1 red bell pepper, chopped
½ cup sugar
½ cup rice wine vinegar (red wine or champagne vinegar will also work)
Salt

Directions

1. Set your immersion circulator to 125°F/51.6°and combine all the ingredients in a vacuum-sealed bag.

2. Seal the bag and immerse in the water bath for 30 minutes.

3. Remove the bag from water and chill in the refrigerator for 1 hour before serving.

13. COCONUT AND ALMOND PORRIDGE

Cal.: 260 | Fat: 12g | Protein: 16g

Preparation Time: 11 minutes
Cooking Time: 3 hours
Servings: 1

Ingredients

½ cup ground almonds
¾ cup coconut cream
1 teaspoon Cinnamon powder
1 teaspoon Stevia
1 pinch ground cardamom
1 pinch ground cloves
1 pinch Nutmeg

Directions

1. Combine all the ingredients in a vacuum-sealed bag.

2. Immerse the bag to the preheated water bath for 3 hours at 180°F/82°C.

3. Remove from the bag, serve, and enjoy.

14. GLAZED CARROTS

Cal.: 67 | Fat: 2.1g | Protein: 0.8g

Preparation Time: 11 minutes
Cooking Time: 1 hour
Servings: 4

Ingredients

1 lb. baby carrots
2 teaspoons butter
2 teaspoons honey
Salt and pepper

Directions

1. Preheat the Sous Vide machine to 185°F/85°C

2. Place all the ingredients in the bag including salt and pepper to taste.

3. Seal and place the bag in your preheated container and set your timer for 1 hour.

4. When the carrots are cooked, put them on a plate to cool for a few minutes, and drizzle with cooking juices.

5. Serve with your main dish.

15. HOT CHILI CHUTNEY

Cal.: 91 | Fat: 0.6g | Protein: 1.7g

Preparation Time: 11 minutes
Cooking Time: 5 hours 50 minutes
Servings: 6

Ingredients

5 medium jalapeños
2 medium red bell peppers
1 medium red onion, chopped
½ tablespoon rosemary
1 bay leaf
½ teaspoon ground cinnamon
1/4 teaspoon sea salt
1/4 teaspoon black pepper
½ cup brown sugar
1 tablespoon balsamic vinegar

Directions

1. Preheat the Sous Vide machine to 182°F/83°C.

2. Roast the peppers under a broiler until the skins are completely charred.

3. Transfer the peppers to a bowl, cover with plastic wrap,

and let sit about 15 to 20 minutes or until cool enough to handle.

4. Peel away the charred outer skins, cut the peppers in half, core, seed and finely chop the flesh.

5. Add peppers and remaining ingredients to a cooking pouch and vacuum seal.

6. Immerse the pouch in a water bath and cook for 5 hours.

7. Remove from the water bath and quick chill by submerging in ice water for 30 minutes.

8. Serve right away, or refrigerate in the pouch, unopened, for up to a week.

16. EGGS WITH AVOCADO TOAST

Cal.: 281 | Fat: 2.1g | Protein: 0.8g

Preparation Time: 6 minutes
Cooking Time: 35 minutes
Servings: 4

Ingredients

4 Eggs
4 slices of toasted bread of your choice
1 Avocado, sliced
Fresh chives
A pinch of salt and pepper

Directions

1. Preheat a water bath to 75°C/167°F.

2. Gently lower all the eggs into the bath, making sure they don't crack.

3. Cook for 15 minutes.

4. Remove the eggs.

5. Put the eggs in an ice bowl (half ice, half water) and hold them there for about 1 minute.

6. Place avocado slices on every toast and crack one egg over each slice. Sprinkle it with chives, salt and pepper.

7. Serve.

17. CINNAMON EGGS

Cal.: 240 | Fat: 12g | Protein: 14g

Preparation Time: 13 minutes
Cooking Time: 40 minutes
Servings: 2

Ingredients

1/3 cup heavy cream
2 eggs
1 tablespoon stevia
Pinch of cinnamon powder

Directions

1. Whisk the ingredients together, add to a bag, seal, and add to the prepared water bath for 30 minutes at 167°F/75°C.

2. When done, divide and enjoy!

18. ASPARAGUS

Cal.: 313 | Fat: 26g | Protein: 13g

Preparation Time: 11 minutes
Cooking Time: 24 minutes
Servings: 4

Ingredients

500 g white asparagus
30 g butter
Zest of one lemon
½ teaspoon each of sugar and salt

Directions

1. Peel the asparagus, cut off the woody end.

2. Put the asparagus in the vacuum bag and vacuum seal together with the lemon zest, butter, salt and sugar.

3. Preheat the water bath to 185°F/85°C and add the asparagus for 30 minutes. This also works with the steamer.

4. When you open the bag, the buttery asparagus is ready.

5. A hollandaise sauce with boiled potatoes goes well with it.

19. LEMON FLAVORED SCALLOPS

Cal.: 100 | Fat: 20g | Protein: 9g

Preparation Time: 5 minutes
Cooking Time: 5 hours 10 minutes
Servings: 4

Ingredients

1 ½ pound scallops
1 cup chicken broth
1 tablespoon capers
1 cup cornstarch
1 garlic clove
1 teaspoon lemon zest
1 tablespoon lemon juice
3 teaspoon butter
2 tablespoon parsley
Salt, pepper as per taste

Directions

1. Take a mixing bowl. Mix the cornstarch with broth, capers, salt, pepper, lemon juice, lemon zest, garlic until it dissolves.

2. Preheat the Sous Vide machine to 195°F/91°C.

3. Take the scallops in a Ziploc bag. Add butter and seal the bag.

4. Place this bag in the water bath for 30 minutes.

5. Boil the broth mixture until it thickens. Add butter and parsley.

6. Place scallops on a serving plate. Add the hot broth and serve.

20. TOMATOES

Cal.: 125 | Fat: 2g | Protein: 0.9g

Preparation Time: 7 minutes
Cooking Time: 47 minutes
Servings: 4

Ingredients

4 medium on-the-vine tomatoes
Kosher salt and freshly ground black pepper
2 tbsp. extra virgin olive oil
2 tbsp. balsamic vinegar, plus more for serving
1 sprig of fresh rosemary, plus more for serving

Directions

1. Preheat the Sous Vide machine to 140°F/60°C.

2. Bring water to a boil in a big pot on high heat. Prepare an ice bath.

3. Slice a small X in the top of each tomato and put them in the water. Allow the tomatoes to cook for around 1 minute, until the skin starts to peel off. Then quickly put the tomatoes in the prepared ice bath.

4. When the tomatoes cool down, take off the skins. Sea-

son the tomatoes with salt and pepper to taste.

5. Place the tomatoes in the bag you're going to use to sous along with the olive oil, balsamic vinegar, and rosemary. Then seal the bag.

6. Place the bag in your preheated water and set the timer for 45 minutes.

7. Place the cooked tomatoes on a plate, sprinkle with a little more balsamic vinegar and top with more rosemary to serve.

21. COLORFUL BELL PEPPER MIX

Cal.: 31 | Fat: 0.4g | Protein: 1g

Preparation Time: 20 minutes
Cooking Time: 15 minutes
Servings: 2

Ingredients

1 red bell pepper, chopped
1 yellow bell pepper, chopped
1 green bell pepper, chopped
1 large orange bell pepper, chopped
Salt to taste

Directions

1. Make a water bath, place a cooker in it, and set it at 183°F/84°C.

2. Place all the bell peppers with salt in a vacuum-sealable bag.

3. Release air by the water displacement method, seal and Immerse in the water bath.

4. Set the timer for 15 minutes.

5. Once the timer has stopped, remove and unseal the bag.

6. Serve bell peppers with its juices as a side dish.

22. ARTICHOKES

Cal.: 368 | Fat: 25.7g | Protein: 10.6g

Preparation Time: 21 minutes
Cooking Time: 1 hour
Servings: 2

Ingredients

4 artichokes, trimmed down to their hearts
1/4 cup premium olive oil
1 tablespoon sea salt

Directions

1. Preheat a water bath to 185°F/85°C.

2. Toss artichokes with all ingredients until well-coated in a large mixing bowl.

3. Place in a vacuum sealable bag and vacuum airtight.

4. Add to the water bath and cook for 1 hour.

5. Serve immediately with your favorite dish.

23. FILIPINO ADOBO CHICKEN

Cal.: 376 | Fat: 21.5g | Protein: 36.8g

Preparation Time: 15 minutes
Cooking Time: 4 hours
Servings: 4

Ingredients

1-½ lbs. chicken thighs and drumstick
6 pieces dried bay leaves
1 cup soy sauce
1 head garlic crushed
1 tablespoon whole peppercorn
1/4 cup vinegar
½ cup chicken broth

Directions

1. Preheat the Sous Vide machine to 155°F/68°C.

2. Place the chicken and all of the other ingredients in the bag.

3. Place the bag in your preheated container and set your timer for 4 hours.

4. Serve chicken with the sauce from the bag.

24. MEDITERRANEAN EGGPLANT LASAGNA

Cal.: 25 | Fat: 0.2g | Protein: 1g

Preparation Time: 20 minutes
Cooking Time: 2 hours
Servings: 3

Ingredients

3 tbsp. yogurt with live active cultures
4 ½ cups plus 3 tbsp. whole milk
8 tbsp. unsalted butter
10 ounces of gingersnap cookies
2 tsp. unflavored powdered gelatin
1 tsp. kosher salt
1 tsp. finely grated lemon zest
½ cup packed light brown sugar
¼ cup granulated sugar
3 cups of fresh blueberries
2 tbsp. minced fresh mint, plus extra for garnish
¼ cup freshly squeezed lemon juice

Directions

1. Preheat the Sous Vide machine to 115°F/46°C.

2. Set a medium saucepan of medium heat. Add in 4 cups of milk and heat to 180°F/82°C. Then, pour the heated milk into a large canning jar and cool to 100-120°F/37-49°C.

3. Add the yogurt into the jar and stir. Seal the jar with a lid and place into the water bath. Cook in the cooker for 24 hours. Cover the water bath with cling wrap to prevent water evaporation. Add a little bit of water from time to time to keep the jar Immersed.

4. Once done, remove the jar carefully from the water bath and place into a bowl filled with ice water to chill. Preheat the oven to 350°F/176°C. Place the salt, butter and gingersnaps in a food processor and pulse until finely ground. Transfer the mixture into a 9-inch pie plate and press the mixture into the bottom and sides to make an even layer of crust. Bake in the oven for 25 minutes or until set. Once done, set aside to cool completely.

5. Whisk together the 3 tablespoons of milk and gelatin in a small bowl. Set aside for 10 minutes. Meanwhile, place the remaining ½ cup milk into a small saucepan set over medium heat. Bring the milk to a simmer then remove from the heat. Whisk in the gelatin mixture into the saucepan. Add in the yogurt, lemon zest and brown sugar. Whisk together until well-combined. Pour the mixture into the cooled pie crust and smooth the top. Place the pie in the refrigerator and chill for 2 hours.

6. Place the lemon juice, granulated sugar and blueberries in a medium saucepan and mix until combined. Bring the mixture to boil then reduce the heat to low. Simmer until the mixture is reduced to half. Remove the saucepan from the heat and stir in the fresh mint.

7. To serve, top the pie with the blueberry sauce and the extra mint leaves.

25. BARBECUE CHICKEN

Cal.: 123 | Fat: 4.8g | Protein: 181.1g

Preparation Time: 10 minutes
Cooking Time: 90 minutes
Servings: 4

Ingredients

4 chicken breasts
1 or 2 sprigs of fresh thyme
1 or 2 sprigs of fresh rosemary
½ teaspoon ancho pepper, or other chili powder
BBQ Sauce

Directions

1. Set your immersion circulator for 141°F/60°C.

2. Season the chicken with salt and pepper and place them in a vacuum-sealed bag.

3. Add the rosemary and thyme to the bag and seal.

4. Place the bag in the water bath and cook for at least 1 ½ hours and not more than 2 ½.

5. When the chicken is almost finished cooking, heat either your grill or broiler too high. Remove the chicken from the bag and pat dry with paper towels.

6. Slather with BBQ sauce and place them on the grill or under the broiler for just long enough to char the sauce. Serve immediately.

26. LEMON PORK CHOPS

Cal.: 286 | Fat: 23.4g | Protein: 18g

Preparation Time: 5 minutes
Cooking Time: 6 hours
Servings: 4

Ingredients

4 pork chops, bone in
1 lemon, sliced
4 fresh thyme sprigs, chopped
1 tbsp. olive oil
Pepper
Salt

Directions

1. Preheat the Sous Vide machine to 138°F/59°C.

2. Season pork chops with pepper and salt.

3. Place pork chops into the Ziploc bag with thyme and lemon slices. Drizzle with olive oil.

4. Remove all air from the bag before sealing.

5. Place the bag into the hot water bath and cook for 6

hours.

6. Remove pork chops from the bag and pat dry with a paper towel.

7. Using a kitchen torch, sear the pork chops until caramelizing.

8. Serve and enjoy!

27. BURGERS

Cal.: 578 | Fat: 39g | Protein: 52g

Preparation Time: 6 minutes
Cooking Time: 1 hour
Servings: 2

Ingredients

10 oz. freshly ground beef
2 hamburger buns
2 slices American cheese
Salt
Pepper
Condiments and toppings of choice

Directions

1. Preheat the Sous Vide machine to 137°F/58.3°C

2. Use your hands to form the burgers into 2 equal-sized 1-inch-thick patties.

3. Place the patties in the bag you're going to use to sous and seal the bag.

4. Place the bag in your preheated water and set the timer for 1 hour.

5. When the patties are ready, heat a skittle (ideally cast-iron) on high heat.

6. When it gets really hot, put in the patties. Let the patties sear for 1 minute, flipping halfway through. When you flip the burgers, top with cheese slices, so the cheese melts.

7. Serve on buns with the condiments of your choice.

28. SPICY HONEY SRIRACHA WINGS

Cal.: 195 | Fat: 9.3g | Protein: 22.3g

Preparation Time: 6 minutes
Cooking Time: 46 minutes
Servings: 4

Ingredients

1 lb. chicken wings
½ teaspoon sea salt
½ teaspoon paprika
½ teaspoon garlic
½ teaspoon ginger
½ teaspoon black pepper

For the glaze:
1 tablespoon sesame oil
2 tablespoons soy sauce
2 tablespoons honey
2 tablespoons Sriracha

Directions

1. Preheat the water bath to 140°F/60°C

2. Mix spices in a mixing bowl and toss wings to coat.

3. Add wings to a vacuum bag.

4. Cook the wings for 40 minutes.

5. Combine glaze ingredients in a large mixing bowl.

6. Transfer chicken wings in an ice bath.

7. For crispy wings, fry in a cast-iron skillet on high heat for 1 to 2 minutes, or until golden.

8. Toss the wings in the glaze and serve hot.

29. FRESH HERB RUBBED PORK CHOPS

Cal.: 518 | Fat: 31g | Protein: 52g

Preparation Time: 11 minutes
Cooking Time: 3 hours
Servings: 3

Ingredients

For the rub:
1/4 cup parsley
10 large basil leaves
1/4 cup rosemary, stems removed
1/4 cup chives
6 sprigs thyme, remove stems
2 garlic cloves, minced
1 zest of 1 lemon
1 tbsp. white balsamic vinegar
½ tsp. salt
1 tsp. fresh cracked pepper
1/4 cup extra virgin olive oil

For the pork:
4 bone in pork chops about 1 ½ inches thick

Directions

1. Preheat the Sous Vide machine to 140°F/60°C.

2. Place the basil, rosemary, chives and thyme in a food processor or blender, and pulse until finely chopped.

3. Add the remaining rub ingredients and blend until the ingredients form a paste.

4. Coat the pork chops with the rub mixture.

5. Place the pork chops in the bag or bags you're going to use to sous, and seal the bag or bags.

6. Place the bag in the preheated water and set the timer for 2 hours.

7. When the pork chops are almost done, preheat your broiler.

8. Coat a rimmed baking sheet with olive oil and place the cooked pork chops on it. Let the pork cook under the broiler for 3 to 4 minutes per side. The pork chops should have a nice brown color and a lightly crisp texture.

9. Serve the pork chops immediately.

30. JUICY ORANGE DUCK BREAST

Cal.: 155 | Fat: 4.2g | Protein: 18g

Preparation Time: 18 minutes
Cooking Time: 10 hours
Servings: 6

Ingredients

19 oz. duck breast, with skin
1 oz. fresh rosemary
1 teaspoon salt
1 teaspoon ground black pepper
½ cup orange juice
2 tablespoon honey
1 tablespoon ghee
½ teaspoon fennel seeds
¼ teaspoon ground cardamom

Directions

1. Cut the duck breast into 2 parts.

2. Then chop the fresh rosemary.

3. Sprinkle the duck breasts with salt, ground black pepper and ground cardamom from each side.

4. After this, sprinkle the duck breasts with fresh rosemary.

5. Then rub the duck breasts with honey and put them in the plastic bags. Use 2 bags to make the taste of every part of the duck breast wonderful.

6. Then add the orange juice.

7. Seal the plastic bags and put them in the preheated to 158°F/69°C water batch.

8. Cook the duck breasts for 10 hours.

9. After this, open the plastic bags and discard the duck breast. Leave the orange juice sauce in the plastic bag.

10. Toss the ghee into the saucepan and melt it.

11. When the ghee starts to boil, add the duck breasts and roast them on high heat for 2 minutes from each side.

12. After this, add the orange juice from the plastic bags.

13. Then add the fennel seeds and reduce the heat to the medium level.

14. Simmer the duck breast for 5 minutes with the closed lid.

15. Then serve the duck breasts with a small amount of the orange juice sauce.

16. Enjoy!

31. CRUNCHY COCONUT SHRIMPS

Cal.: 260 | Fat: 14g | Protein: 7g

Preparation Time: 5 minutes
Cooking Time: 5 hours 10 minutes
Servings: 4

Ingredients

24 shrimps
1/4 cup skim milk
3 tablespoon flour
½ cup coconut
1/4 cup cornflakes

Directions

1. Preheat the Sous Vide machine to 195°F/91°C.

2. Take the shrimps in a Ziploc bag and apply a vacuum to remove the air.

3. Place this bag in the water bath for 5 minutes.

4. Make a mixture of milk and flour in a mixing bowl. Toss the above shrimps in it.

5. In another mixing bowl, make a mixture of coconut and cornflakes crumbs.

6. Add the shrimps to the above mixture and coat it uniformly.

7. Preheat the oven to 450 ° F. Grease the baking tray with cooking spray.

8. Place the shrimps on this tray and bake for 5 minutes. Flip and repeat.

9. Serve hot.

32. HADDOCK ON VEGETABLE SAUCE

Cal.: 349 | Fat: 19g | Protein: 27g

Preparation Time: 11 minutes
Cooking Time: 3 hours
Servings: 3

Ingredients

4 6oz. haddock fillets

Marinade:
1 pinch curry
1 pinch brown sugar
1 pinch fine sea salt
5 tablespoons olive oil
1 sprig thyme, chopped
1 teaspoon lemon juice

Vegetables:
1 pinch chili powder
1 cucumber
3 carrots
1 leek, chopped
1 tablespoon olive oil
3 bell peppers, red, yellow, and green
1 sweet potato
Salt, and pepper, to taste

Directions

1. Preheat the Sous Vide machine to 130°F/55°C.

2. In a bag, combine marinade ingredients.

3. Add haddock fillets and shake to coat the fish.

4. Vacuum seal the bag and cook for 30 minutes.

5. In a separate bag, combine all vegetables, with seasonings and olive oil. Vacuum seal the bag and cook the veggies at 185°F/85°C for 40 minutes.

6. Open the bags carefully.

7. Heat some olive oil in a large skillet. Cook the fish fillets for 2 minutes per side.

8. Serve fish with vegetables.

33. LOBSTER TAIL

Cal.: 368 | Fat: 38g | Protein: 23g

Preparation Time: 11 minutes
Cooking Time: 3 hours
Servings: 2

Ingredients

2 Lobster tails (frozen)
10 Tbsp. butter
1 Tbsp. fresh parsley

Directions

1. Preheat the water bath to 134°F/56°C.

2. Defrost lobster tails in a bowl of water for approximately 30 minutes.

3. Cut the shell down the middle with kitchen shears and slowly but firmly pull the shell apart, ensuring not to rip the meat.

4. Remove lobster meat from the shell and devein, if necessary.

5. Place lobster tails, fresh parsley and 2-3 tbsp. of butter into a heavy duty Ziploc bag.

6. Use the water displacement method to remove the air from the bag and seal it.

7. Place the bag in the water bath and cook for 1 hour.

8. Melt 6-8 tbsp. of butter in a saucepan over medium heat.

9. When melted, pour the butter into a serving bowl.

10. Serve.

34. SEA BASS

Cal.: 362 | Fat: 36g | Protein: 16g

Preparation Time: 18 minutes
Cooking Time: 30 minutes
Servings: 2

Ingredients

2 sea bass portions, each weighing 120g
2 lemon wedges
Dash of olive oil
Pinch of sea salt

Directions

1. Preheat the water bath to a temperature of 122°F/50°C.

2. Sprinkle the sea salt over the sea bass and seal in a vacuum bag with olive oil and lemon wedges.

3. Place the bag in the water bath and cook for 15 minutes.

4. When it is finished cooking, carefully slide the cooked fish out of the vacuum bag, and pat dry.

5. Heat a skillet on high heat. Sear on the skin side until the skin is crisp and golden.

6. Serve.

35. CAJUN SPICED TILAPIA

Cal.: 188 | Fat: 7.3g | Protein: 22.9g

Preparation Time: 11 minutes
Cooking Time: 30 minutes
Servings: 4

Ingredients

4 tilapia fillets
1 tablespoon black pepper
1 tablespoon kosher salt
1 tablespoon smoked paprika
2 tbsp. Italian seasoning
2 tbsp. cayenne pepper
2 tbsp. garlic powder
2 tbsp. dried onion granules or onion powder
1 tablespoon vegetable oil

Directions

1. Preheat the Sous Vide machine to 138°F/59°C. Pat the fish dry using a paper towel.

2. Mix together all the spices in a bowl and rub the spice mixture on the fish.

3. Place the fish in the bag and cook for 30 minutes.

4. Heat the oil in a skillet over medium-high heat and add the fish to the pan-searing for 1 minute per side.

5. Serve.

36. BRINED SALMON

Cal.: 399 | Fat: 28.8g | Protein: 24g

Preparation Time: 5 hours 11 minutes
Cooking Time: 28 minutes
Servings: 4

Ingredients

4 salmon fillets
6 tbsp. unsalted butter
3 tbsp. sugar
Fresh ground pepper
5 tablespoon coarse salt, plus more for taste
½ cup olive oil or melted, cooled butter

Directions

1. Place 4 ½ cups of water in a large bowl. Pour in the 5 tbsp. salt and 3 tbsp. sugar. Stir the mixture until all solids dissolve. Place the salmon in the mixture and Immerse. Place the bowl in the refrigerator for 5 hours.

2. Preheat the Sous Vide machine to 115°F/46°C. Take the salmon out of the bowl and place it in separate bags along with 2 tbsp. olive oil.

3. Place the bags in your preheated container and set your timer for 24 minutes.

4. In the last few minutes of cooking, place the 6 tbsp. butter in a skillet and melt it over medium-low heat.

5. When the salmon is cooked, salt and pepper to taste. Place the salmon in the skillet and allow it to cook for 30 seconds per side. Serve immediately.

37. MARINATED KING PRAWNS WITH LIME MAYONNAISE

Cal.: 428 | Fat: 38g | Protein: 20g

Preparation Time: 11 minutes
Cooking Time: 61 hours
Servings: 8

Ingredients

16 fresh king prawns
30 g of fish sauce
2 fresh green chilies
Sesame
2 limes in juice
5 g of ginger
5 g of garlic
1 mini lime
Soya
Egg white
Rice noodles
Flour

For Mayonnaise:
10 units of lime leaves
250 g of sunflower oil
1 egg
Salt, to taste
Juice of a mini lime

Directions

1. First, mix the ingredients for the marinade: the fish sauce, the chopped chilies, lime and mini lime juice, chopped ginger, garlic and soya.

2. Peel the king prawns leaving the tail and removing the head.

3. Marinate the king prawns by vacuum packing for 20 minutes, which will accelerate the marinating.

4. Preheat the water bath to 140°F/60°C.

5. Once the king prawns are marinated, remove the solid elements and put them aside.

6. For the mayonnaise, place oil and lime leaves in a Ziploc bag and seal using the water displacement method.

7. Immerse the bag, and cook for 1 hour.

8. When the oil is finished cooking, make a basic mayonnaise with the egg, the lime oil, the mini lime juice and salt.

9. Meanwhile, break up the rice noodles by hand leaving pieces of 1–2cm.

10. To finish, cover the king prawns with flour, beaten egg white and finally the broken rice noodles. Fry in an abundance of hot oil.

11. Serve with the mayonnaise.

38. CILANTRO CURRIED ZUCCHINIS

Cal.: 17 | Fat: 0.3g | Protein: 1.2g

Preparation Time: 10 minutes
Cooking Time: 25 minutes
Servings: 3

Ingredients

3 small zucchinis, diced
2 tsp. curry powder
1 tbsp. olive oil
Salt to taste
Pepper to taste
¼ cup cilantro

Directions

1. Make a water bath, place a cooker in it, and set it at 185°F/85°C.

2. Place the zucchinis in a vacuum-sealable bag.

3. Release air by the water displacement method, seal and Immerse the bag in the water bath. Set the timer for 20 minutes.

4. Once the timer has stopped, remove and unseal the bag.

5. Place a skillet over medium, add olive oil.

6. Once it has heated, add the zucchinis and the remaining listed ingredients.

7. Season with salt and stir-fry for 5 minutes.

8. Serve.

39. BEEF SHOGAYAKI

Cal.: 498 | Fat: 41.1g | Protein: 67g

Preparation Time: 11 minutes
Cooking Time: 12 hours
Servings: 3

Ingredients

18 oz. Beef Stew Meat
3 tbsp. Soy Sauce
3 tbsp. Mirin
3 tbsp. Water
1 Thumb-Sized Piece Ginger grated
1 tbsp. high-smoke point oil

Directions

1. Preheat the Sous Vide machine to 140°F/60°C.

2. Mix together the soy, water, ginger and mirin in a bowl. Add the beef, and toss it in the mixture to coat.

3. Place the beef in the bag you're going to use to sous along with the sauce and seal the bag.

4. Place the bag in your preheated water and set the timer for 12 hours.

5. When the beef is ready, heat a skittle (ideally cast-iron) on high heat.

6. When it gets really hot, pour in the oil and put in the beef. Let the steak sear for 1 minute, flipping halfway through. The steak should form a nice crust on both sides.

40. VANILLA PEARS

Cal.: 160 | Fat: 0.2g | Protein: 0.5g

Preparation Time: 15 minutes
Cooking Time: 30 minutes
Servings: 2

Ingredients

2 Comice pears
1/4 cup sugar syrup
1 vanilla pod, cracked

Directions

1. Prepare and preheat the water bath at 170°F/76°C.

2. Add pears and all the ingredients to a zipper-lock bag.

3. Seal the zipper-lock bag using the water immersion method.

4. Place the sealed bag in the bath and cook for 30 minutes.

5. Once done, transfer the pears to a plate and slice them.

6. Strain the remaining sauce and pour over the pears.

7. Serve.

41. PEACH

Cal.: 374 | Fat: 23g | Protein: 14g

Preparation Time: 9 minutes
Cooking Time: 2 hours
Servings: 2

Ingredients

2 peaches or apricots
60 g cane sugar
1 tbsp. freshly roasted almond sticks
Juice of ½ lemon
50 ml of water
1 teaspoon cinnamon
1 teaspoon vanilla sugar

Directions

1. Melt cane and vanilla sugar, 40 ml water and cinnamon in a pan at 212°F/100°C for 4 minutes to form a sauce.

2. In the meantime, remove the core of the peaches and quarter them.

3. Mix the sauce with the fruit and let it work for a moment.

4. Vacuum the peaches with a little sauce and place them in a water bath that has been heated to 176°F/80°C. Cook the peach pieces for 90 minutes.

5. Divide the peaches between 2 plates, pour the remaining sauce over them and sprinkle with the freshly roasted almond sticks.

42. ROSE WATER APRICOTS

Cal.: 17 | Fat: 0.2g | Protein: 0.5g

Preparation Time: 11 minutes
Cooking Time: 60 minutes
Servings: 8

Ingredients

8 apricots
1 tsp. rosewater
½ cup water

Directions

1. Preheat your Sous Vide Machine to 180°F/82°C. Cut the apricots in half and remove the pit.

2. Place all the ingredients in a bag. Then, place the bag in your preheated container and set your timer for 1 hour.

3. When the peaches are cooked, serve in a small bowl or plate.

43. PEACH AND ORANGE JAM

Cal.: 50 | Fat: 0.5g | Protein: 0.1g

Preparation Time: 11 minutes
Cooking Time: 2 hours
Servings: 10

Ingredients

2 cups peaches, coarsely chopped
1 ½ cup white sugar
1 cup water
Zest and juice of 1 orange

Directions

1. Preheat the Sous Vide machine to 190°F/88°C

2. Put the ingredients into the vacuum bag and seal it.

3. Cook for 2 hours in the water bath.

4. Serve over ice cream or cake, or store in the fridge in an airtight container.

44. PINEAPPLE IN MALIBU

Cal.: 110 | Fat: 0.1g | Protein: 0.5g

Preparation Time: 15 minutes
Cooking Time: 2 hours
Servings: 4

Ingredients

1 pineapple, peeled and sliced
4 tablespoons of Malibu
1 teaspoon coriander seeds, toasted
1/4 cup brown sugar

Directions

1. Prepare and preheat the water bath at 185°F/85°C.

2. Add pineapple and all the ingredients to a zipper-lock bag.

3. Seal the zipper-lock bag using the water immersion method.

4. Place the sealed bag in the bath and cook for 2 hours.

5. Once done, transfer the pineapple to a plate.

6. Serve.

45. SWEET CORN CHEESECAKE

Cal.: 443 | Fat: 34.5g | Protein: 11g

Preparation Time: 15 minutes
Cooking Time: 90 minutes
Servings: 5

Ingredients

2 (8-oz) packages of cream cheese
100 grams granulated sugar
2 grams kosher salt
3 whole eggs
5 grams vanilla extract
130 grams buttermilk, or heavy whipping cream
5 (8-oz) mason jars

Directions

1. Preheat your Sous Vide Machine to 176°F/80°C. Allow the cream cheese to rise to room temperature.

2. Put the cream cheese, salt and sugar in a food processor. Process until smooth, making sure you scrape the sides of the bowl throughout to ensure all ingredients are mixed.

3. Put in the eggs and vanilla and follow the same process as last time.

4. While the food processor is running, pour in the buttermilk. Continue to process until smooth. Strain the mixture through a fine-mesh sieve for the smoothest texture. Pour an equal amount of mixture into each jar.

5. Tighten the lids so they're finger tight, but not fully airtight to prevent cracking of the jars.

6. Put the jars in your preheated container and set your timer for 90 minutes.

7. When the cheesecake is cooked, place the jars on a kitchen towel on the counter. Let the jars come to room temperature. Refrigerate overnight.

8. Serve with your favorite toppings.

46. BANANAS FOSTER

Cal.: 772 | Fat: 40.4g | Protein: 5.4g

Preparation Time: 15 minutes
Cooking Time: 26 minutes
Servings: 2

Ingredients

2 tbsp. dark rum
4 tbsp. butter
1 tsp. vanilla
½ cup brown sugar
2 bananas
1 tsp. cinnamon
½ cup pecans
2 scoops of vanilla ice cream

Directions

1. Preheat your Sous Vide Machine to 145°F/63°C. Peel and cut the bananas into 1-inch pieces.

2. Place the vanilla, butter, brown sugar and rum in a pan over high heat. Bring the mixture to a boil and remove from heat.

3. Season the bananas with cinnamon and put them in

the bag of your choice with 3 tbsp. of the sauce.

4. Place the bag in your preheated container and set your timer for 25 minutes.

5. When the bananas are cooked, plate them with a scoop of vanilla ice cream and top with the remaining sauce.

6. Serve immediately.

47. VANILLA ICE CREAM

Cal.: 290 | Fat: 7g | Protein: 20g

Preparation Time: 18 minutes
Cooking Time: 5 hours
Servings: 4

Ingredients

6 Egg Yolks
½ cup Brown Sugar
1 ½ tsp. Vanilla Extract
2 cups Half and Half

Directions

1. Preheat the Sous Vide machine to 180°F/82°C.

2. In your food processor, whisk all of the ingredients together until smooth and creamy, and place in a Ziploc bag.

3. Seal the bag and immerse in the preheated.

4. Cook for 1 hour. Make sure there are no clumps before transferring the mixture to a container with a lid.

5. Remove and unseal the bag. Let cool in an ice bath. Pour the mixture into an ice cream machine, and process according to the maker's instructions.

6. Place in the freezer for 4 hours until firm. Scoop into bowls and serve.

48. FEISTY KIWI AND VANILLA

Cal.: 148 | Fat: 5g | Protein: 5g

Preparation Time: 8 minutes
Cooking Time: 20 hour
Servings: 4

Ingredients

2 kiwis, peeled and sliced
2 tablespoons granulated sugar
1 tablespoon fresh lemon, squeezed
Fresh mint leaves

Directions

1. Prepare your water bath by dipping the immersion circulator and increasing the temperature to 176°F/80°C.

2. Take a medium bowl and add kiwi slices, sugar, lemon juice and stir.

3. Transfer the mixture to a zip bag and seal using the immersion method.

4. Cook for 20 minutes and remove the bag from the water.

5. Divide the mixture between 2 serving plates.

6. Scoop yogurt/vanilla ice cream onto the plate next to your kiwi and garnish with some mint leaves.

7. Serve!

49. JUICY RASPBERRIES

Cal.: 75 | Fat: 0.5g | Protein: 0.8g

Preparation Time: 15 minutes
Cooking Time: 2 hours
Servings: 4

Ingredients

2 cups fresh raspberries
2 tablespoons elderflower cordial
1 tablespoon apple juice
1 teaspoon cornstarch

Directions

1. Prepare and preheat the water bath at 150°F/65°C.

2. Add raspberries and all the ingredients to a zipper-lock bag.

3. Seal the zipper-lock bag using the water immersion method.

4. Place the sealed bag in the bath and cook for 2 hours.

5. Once done, transfer the raspberries to a plate and slice them.

6. Serve.

50. MINI CHEESECAKES

Cal.: 380 | Fat: 16g | Protein: 19g

Preparation Time: 7 minutes
Cooking Time: 1 hour 40 minutes
Servings: 3

Ingredients

3 eggs
5 tbsp. cottage cheese
½ cup cream cheese
4 tbsp. sugar
½ tsp. vanilla extract

Directions

1. Place all of the ingredients in a mixing bowl. Beat with an electric mixer for a few minutes, until soft and smooth. Divide the mixture between 3 mason jars. Seal.

2. Preheat the Sous Vide machine to 175°F/79°C. Immerse the jars inside the bath. Cook for 90 minutes. Chill and serve with your favourite toppings.

TEMPERATURE CHARTS

🥩 MEAT	°F 🌡 TEMPERATURE	⏱ TIME
Beef Steak, rare	129 °F	1 hour 30 min.
Beef Steak, medium-rare	136 °F	1 hour 30min.
Beef Steak, well done	158 °F	1 hour 30min.
Beef Roast, rare	133 °F	7 hours
Beef Roast, medium-rare	140 °F	6 hours
Beef Roast, well done	158 °F	5 hours
Beef Tough Cuts, rare	136 °F	24 hours
Beef Tough Cuts, medium-rare	149 °F	16 hours
Beef Tough Cuts, well done	185 °F	8 hours
Lamb Tenderloin, Rib eye, T-bone, Cutlets	134 °F	4 hours
Lamb Roast, Leg	134 °F	10 hours
Lamb Flank Steak, Brisket	134 °F	12 hours
Pork Chop, rare	136 °F	1 hour
Pork Chop, medium-rare	144 °F	1 hour
Pork Chop, well done	158 °F	1 hour
Pork Roast, rare	136 °F	3 hours

🥩 MEAT	°F🌡 TEMPERATURE	⏱ TIME
Pork Roast, medium-rare	144 °F	3 hours
Pork Roast, well done	158 °F	3 hours
Pork Tough Cuts, rare	144 °F	16 hours
Pork Tough Cuts, medium-rare	154 °F	12 hours
Pork Tough Cuts, well done	154 °F	8 hours
Pork Tenderloin	134 °F	1 hour 30min
Pork Baby Back Ribs	165 °F	6 hours
Pork Cutlets	134 °F	5 hours
Pork Spare Ribs	160 °F	12 hours
Pork Belly (quick)	185 °F	5 hours
Pork Belly (slow)	167 °F	24 hours

🐟 FISH AND SEAFOOD	°F🌡 TEMPERATURE	⏱ TIME
Fish, tender	104 °F	40 min.
Fish, tender and flaky	122 °F	40 min.
Fish, well done	140 °F	40 min.
Salmon, Tuna, Trout, Mackerel, Halibut, Snapper, Sole	126 °F	30 min.
Lobster	140 °F	50 min.
Scallops	140 °F	50 min.
Shrimp	140 °F	35 min.

🍗 POULTRY	°F 🌡 TEMPERATURE	⏱ TIME
Chicken White Meat, super-supple	140 °F	2 hours
Chicken White Meat, tender and juicy	149 °F	1 hour
Chicken White Meat, well done	167 °F	1 hour
Chicken Breast, bone-in	146 °F	2 hours 30 min.
Chicken Breast, boneless	146 °F	1 hour
Turkey Breast, bone-in	146 °F	4 hours
Turkey Breast, boneless	146 °F	2 hours 30 min.
Duck Breast	134 °F	1 hour 30 min.
Chicken Dark Meat, tender	149 °F	1 hour 30 min.
Chicken Dark Meat, falling off the bone	167 °F	1 hour 30 min.
Chicken Leg or Thigh, bone-in	165 °F	4 hours
Chicken Thigh, boneless	165 °F	1 hour
Turkey Leg or Thigh	165 °F	2 hours
Duck Leg	165 °F	8 hours
Split Game Hen	150 °F	6 hours

🥕 VEGETABLES	°F 🌡 TEMPERATURE	⏱ TIME
Vegetables, root (carrots, potato, parsnips, beets, celery root, turnips)	183 °F	3 hours
Vegetables, tender (asparagus, broccoli, cauliflower, fennel, onions, pumpkin, eggplant, green beans, corn)	183 °F	1 hour
Vegetables, greens (kale, spinach, collard greens, Swiss chard)	183 °F	3 min.

🍐 FRUITS	°F 🌡 TEMPERATURE	⏱ TIME
Fruit, firm (apple, pear)	183 °F	45 min.
Fruit, for purée	185 °F	30 min.
Fruit, berries for topping desserts (blueberries, blackberries, raspberries, strawberries, cranberries)	154 °F	30 min.

WHAT TEMPERATURE SHOULD BE USED?

The rule of thumb is that the thicker the piece, the longer it should cook. Higher temperatures shorten the cooking time. Lower temperatures may take longer.

	TEMPERATURE	MIN COOKING TIME	MAX COOKING TIME
EGGS			
Soft Yolk	140°F (60°C)	1 hour	1 hour
Creamy Yolk	145°F (63°C)	¾ hour	1 hour
GREEN VEGETABLES			
Rare	183°F (84°C)	¼ hour	¾ hour
ROOTS			
Rare	183°F (84°C)	1 hour	3 hours
FRUITS			
Warm	154°F (68°C)	1¾ hour	2½ hour
Soft Fruits	185°F (85°C)	½ hour	1½ hour

	TEMPERATURE	MIN COOKING TIME	MAX COOKING TIME
CHICKEN			
Rare	140°F (60°C)	1 hour	3 hours
Medium	150°F (65°C)	1 hour	3 hours
Well Done	167°F (75°C)	1 hour	3 hours
BEEF STEAK			
Rare	130°F (54°C)	1½ hours	3 hours
Medium	140°F (60°C)	1½ hours	3 hours
Well Done	145°F (63°C)	1½ hours	3 hours
ROAST BEEF			
Rare	133°F (54°C)	7 hours	16 hours
Medium	140°F (60°C)	6 hours	14 hours
Well Done	158°F (70°C)	5 hours	11 hours
PORK CHOP BONE-IN			
Rare	136°F (58°C)	1 hour	4 hours
Medium	144°F (62°C)	1 hour	4 hours
Well Done	158°F (70°C)	1 hour	4 hours
PORK LOIN			
Rare	136°F (58°C)	3 hours	5½ hours
Medium	144°F (62°C)	3 hours	5 hours
Well Done	158°F (70°C)	3 hours	3½ hours
FISH			
Tender	104°F (40°C)	½ hour	½ hour
Medium	124°F (51°C)	½ hour	1 hour
Well Done	131°F (55°C)	½ hour	1½ hours

COOKING CONVERSION

TEMPERATURE CONVERSIONS	
CELSIUS	FAHRENHEIT
54.5°C	130°F
60.0°C	140°F
65.5°C	150°F
71.1°C	160°F
76.6°C	170°F
82.2°C	180°F
87.8°C	190°F
93.3°C	200°F
100°C	212°F

WEIGHT COVERSION

½ oz.	15g
1 oz.	30g
2 oz.	60g
3 oz.	85g
4 oz.	110g
5 oz.	140g
6 oz.	170g
7 oz.	200g
8 oz.	225g
9 oz.	255g
10 oz.	280g
11 oz.	310g
12 oz.	340g
13 oz.	370g
14 oz.	400g
15 oz.	425g
1 lb.	450g

LIQUID VOLUME CONVERSION		
CUPS / TABLESPOONS	FL. OUNCES	MILLILITERS
1 cup	8 fl. Oz.	240 ml
¾ cup	6 fl. Oz.	180 ml
2/3 cup	5 fl. Oz.	150 ml
½ cup	4 fl. Oz.	120 ml
1/3 cup	2 ½ fl. Oz.	75 ml
¼ cup	2 fl. Oz.	60 ml
1/8 cup	1 fl. Oz.	30 ml
1 tablespoon	½ fl. Oz.	15 ml

TEASPOON (tsp.) / TABLESPOON (Tbsp.)	MILLILITERS
1 tsp.	5ml
2 tsp.	10ml
1 Tbsp.	15ml
2 Tbsp.	30ml
3 Tbsp.	45ml
4 Tbsp.	60ml
5 Tbsp.	75ml
6 Tbsp.	90ml
7 Tbsp.	105ml

LIQUID VOLUME MEASUREMENTS			
TABLE-SPOONS	TEASPOONS	FLUID OUNCES	CUPS
16	48	8 fl. Oz.	1
12	36	6 fl. Oz.	¾
8	24	4 fl. Oz.	½
5 ½	16	2 2/3 fl. Oz.	1/3
4	12	2 fl. Oz.	¼
1	3	0.5 fl. Oz.	1/16

RECIPE INDEX

A Bed of Vegetables 14
Artichokes 48
Asparagus 41
Bananas Foster 92
Barbecue Chicken 52
Beef Shogayaki 80
Brined Salmon 74
Brioche and Eggs 24
Burgers 56
Cajun Spiced Tilapia 72
Cilantro Curried Zucchinis 78
Cinnamon Eggs 40
Citrus Yogurt 26
Coconut and Almond Porridge 33
Colorful Bell Pepper Mix 46
Crunchy Coconut Shrimps 64
Dungeness Crab 29
Eggs with Avocado Toast 38
Feisty Kiwi and Vanilla 96
Filipino Adobo Chicken 49
Fresh Herb Rubbed Pork Chops 60
Garlic Corn and Herby 20
Glazed Carrots 34
Haddock on Vegetable Sauce 66

Hot Chili Chutney	36
Juicy Orange Duck Breast	62
Juicy Raspberries	98
Lemon Flavored Scallops	42
Lemon Hummus	12
Lemon Pork Chops	54
Lobster Tail	68
Marinated King Prawns with Lime Mayonnaise	76
Mediterranean Eggplant Lasagna	50
Mini Cheesecakes	100
Nuts, Beetroot and Cheese Salad	22
Orange Yogurt	28
Peach	84
Peach and Orange Jam	87
Pineapple in Malibu	88
Rose Water Apricots	86
Sea Bass	70
Shrimp and Avocado Salsa	18
Spicy Honey Sriracha Wings	58
Summer Salsa	32
Sweet Corn Cheesecake	90
Tomato And Mango Salsa	16
Tomatoes	44
Vanilla Ice Cream	94
Vanilla Pears	82
Zucchini Medallions	30

www.ingramcontent.com/pod-product-compliance
Lightning Source LLC
Chambersburg PA
CBHW070101120526
44589CB00033B/1459